Stylish Weddings & Things Guide to Developing Your Wedding Budget

By Sherries L. Pritchard

Stylish Weddings & Things Guide to Developing Your Wedding Budget

Copyright © 2013 Sherries L. Pritchard

Stylish Weddings & Things, LLC
Pompton Lakes, New Jersey
www.stylishweddingsandthings.com

DEDICATION

This book is dedicated to my amazing husband Phil and my wonderful children Shamar, Phillip, and Isabella who have been and continue to be extremely loving and supportive of me through this journey of providing engaged couples with assistance in planning their weddings. You guys mean the world to me and I love you very much. Special thanks to my business coach and mentor, Tami Briggs and best friend KJ. Thank you so much for believing in me and pushing me forward. You rock!

FOREWORD

Congratulations on your engagement and welcome to "*Stylish Weddings & Things Guide to Developing Your Wedding Budget*" 10 week course. What an exciting time this is for you and I'm so glad you're here to join other nearly-weds in this wedding planning learning experience. I'm even more thrilled that I can help you plan one of the most important days of your life.

This book is intended to help you get your finances in order so that you can begin planning your wedding on a budget of any size but more specifically on a budget on a small scale. During your search for wedding planning assistance, you'll find countless number of books, blogs, and articles to help you plan your wedding on a budget, but you won't find anything with a primary focus on developing your wedding budget until you read this book.

So let's get you down the aisle in style and on budget! This course will be jam packed with information and tools to help you create a realistic budget for your stylish wedding. If at any time you have any questions related to the "*Stylish Weddings & Things Guide to Developing Your Wedding Budget*", feel free to send me a note to hotline@stylishweddingsandthings.com.

I applaud you for taking the first step into saving your wallet, your bank accounts, and your financial future.

Sincerely,
Sherries Pritchard, CWP

CONTENTS

WEEK 1 – BUDGET PLANNING 4

First thing's first! *Open an Interest Bearing Checking Account for your Wedding Expenses* 4

WEEK 2 – PRIORITIZE 5

Prioritize *YOUR unique budget plan* 5

WEEK 3 - FINANCING YOUR WEDDING 7

Budget Development: *who is paying for your wedding?* 7

WEEK 4 – WHO'S COMING TO YOUR WEDDING 9

Budget Development: *The Guest List Impacts the Budget* 9

WEEK 5 – SHOP WITH PURPOSE 11

Create a Shopping Schedule 11

WEEK 6 – BUDGET FRIENDLY WEDDING PROFESSIONALS 12

Choosing *Your Team* 12

WEEK 7 – ARE YOU DOING IT YOURSELF? 13

When to do it yourself & *When to hire a pro* 13

WEEK 8 – DON'T HAGGLE, YOU'LL GET WHAT YOU PAY FOR & MORE 16

"Vendors will be happy to extend more value in a service than to offer you a discount." 17

WEEK 9 – MONEY SAVING OPTIONS 18

Save more than just *A Few Dollars* 18

WEEK 10 – HONEYMOON TIP 20

Honeymoon Planning *A bit of advice* 20

BONUS – REWARD YOURSELF 21

Reward Yourself, *You Deserve it* 21

APPENDIX 22

First thing's first! *Open an Interest Bearing Checking Account for your Wedding Expenses*

Do this for the sole purpose of keeping your wedding dollar ducks in a row. By having a dedicated wedding checking account, you'll be able to keep a great record of everything you've bought, have a real-time balance of what's available for spending, and you won't dip into your personal accounts meant to sustain your livelihood.

If both of your employers have direct deposit, speak with the payroll administrator about depositing either a percentage of your salaries or a flat dollar amount into your wedding account. This way, you won't have to guess each pay cycle how much either one of you can put in. It will already have been determined and deposited on payday.

Homework Assignment: **This week, take some time to research the different options banks have to offer and compare them side by side. Some checking accounts are interest bearing, which means, if you're planning a wedding for more than a year from now, your wedding checking account can make you some extra cash!**

Welcome to week two of "Stylish Weddings & Things Guide to Developing Your Wedding Budget." In week one, we talked about beginning this process on the right track by setting aside a dedicated bank account to keep track of your wedding related expenses and spending. If you haven't done that yet, I encourage you to not move forward with your budget planning until you have at least put a discipline in place that will discourage you from tapping into your personal, day-to-day, finances.

Every budget template available is not a one size fits all solution to financially plan out your wedding. Today we'll go over the standard wedding expense categories and you will prioritize your budget according to what's important to the two of you. This will be extremely helpful when you begin to develop your budget next week.

Let's begin our next topic…

Prioritize *YOUR unique budget plan*

When you close your eyes and imagine your wedding day, what do you see? What elements jump out at you that make you smile the most? Is it your wedding dress? Is it the décor? Is it the entertainment? Are your guests having a great time? This is an important exercise to do BEFORE you sit down and allocate dollars and cents to your wedding budget because you will, with purpose, have a clear list of your priorities already in order.

We believe that there is no one size fits all budgets when it comes to your wedding. What may be important to one couple is not necessarily the same importance to another. Below is a sample chart we use when consulting with our couples in determining their budget expenditures based on the couples priorities. Place the category items in the order of what means the most to you and give it a percentage value where the grand total is 100%. When you're done, transfer the results in the provided priorities checklist at the end of this book and take with you when you have your budget development meeting (discussed in week 3).

Expense	Priority
Ceremony	
Reception (Venue)	
Reception (Food & Beverage)	
Wedding cake	
Attire	
Décor	
Music	
Photos/Video	
Invitations and other Stationery	
Wedding rings	
Transportation	
Gifts	
Honeymoon	

Homework Assignment: *Close your eyes and imagine what your wedding day would look like. What are the key elements that jump out at you? Write them down and use the priorities check list to record your vision. Take your time with this exercise. Need inspiration? Visit us on Pinterest at www.pinterest.com/StylishWedThing*

Welcome to week three of the "Stylish Weddings & Things Guide to Developing Your Wedding Budget." In week two, we worked together to put your priorities in place so that you can begin the budget development process with purpose. Now you have a clear indication of how you will allocate your wedding dollars.

Ok, so let's begin our next topic…

Budget Development: *who is paying for your wedding?*

This is a very important question that you must have a solid answer to BEFORE you begin planning your wedding if you're not financing it yourselves. Find out who's contributing and how much control of your wedding is attached to their contribution. Knowing who these people are BEFORE you begin developing your budget is crucial to the overall planning process.

Here is a guide to who traditionally pays for what in weddings. It is not the beginning and end all to who should pay, but is helpful when crossing this bridge and can aide you with tactfully approaching your families for financial assistance. Use our wedding budget planner at the end of the book as a guide.

Bride and family traditionally pay for the following expenses:
- Bride's attire and accessories
- Groom's ring
- Invitations and other stationery
- Reception costs
- All of the entertainment
- Bridal party flowers (corsages, bouquets, and boutonnieres)
- Gifts for bridal party and parents
- Photography/Videography

- Décor' and favors
- Out of town guests gifts and accommodations
- Wedding cake

Groom and family traditionally pay for the following expenses:
- Officiant
- Bride's ring & flowers
- Groom's attire and accessories
- Transportation
- Rehearsal Dinner
- Honeymoon

Bridal party traditionally pays for the following expenses:
- Bachelor and Bachelorette parties
- Bridal Shower – Maid of Honor
- Wedding attire and accessories

The second major consideration in pre-planning that significantly affects your budget is how many people you plan to be in attendance. This includes your bridal party, as well as your guests. The more people you invite, consider the food, the drinks, the favors, table décor, etc. and the expenses involved. We'll talk more about managing your budget and guest list in week 4.

Homework Assignment: **Arrange to have your budget meeting with those involved in planning your wedding, using our wedding budget planner and your priorities checklist as a guide. Serve some yummy munchies, keep an open mind, and have fun!**

Welcome to week four of, "Stylish Weddings & Things Guide to Developing Your Wedding Budget." I know what you're thinking, more financial matters! But hey, getting those financial ducks in a row will guarantee you will have a stylish wedding and within budget. So it's critical that we get you in tip top shape before we start spending. Remember, if at any time you have questions or concerns just shoot me an email at hotline@stylishweddingsandthings.com.

Ok, so let's begin our next topic…

Budget Development: *The Guest List Impacts the Budget*

Are you ready to develop your budget? Now that you've prioritized your needs, have a total dollar amount for your wedding, and know who will be helping financially (if anyone), let's populate your budget. You can use the wedding budget template found at the end of this book or download an editable version at www.stylishweddingsandthings.com and add on additional categories as needed.

Take a look at the following categories: Food & Beverage, Stationery, Décor, and Favors Where are these on your priority chart? Each item in these categories is affected by the number of guests you invite. Costs are affected as follows:

Food & Beverage – charged by the person. To get an idea of what you can expect to pay for catering or a venue with all inclusive services, divide the budget amount by the number of guests and you will yield your budgeted per person amount. So, if you have your eyes on a caterer/venue that is more than what you have budgeted, you will need to scale your guest list or increase your budget.

Stationery – usually there is a flat fee for the first allotment of 100 pieces for Save the Dates and Invitations, and you pay additional in bulks of 25 (typically). There are extra fees for insertions like RSVP and direction cards. Don't forget postage costs!

Décor – for every guest you invite, there are seats and tables needed for them. For each table, you'll have to take into account the centerpieces, linens, and place setting elements including guest favors.

Not listed above are FLOWERS which I actually intended on leaving out for purposes of including them with the décor category. HOWEVER, when you have a large bridal party, the personal flowers can add up so I'm mentioning this to you to keep this in mind also. Limiting the amount of people in your bridal party helps reduce costs as well.

How much is your budget by the way? Want to learn a quick and easy way to determine how many people to have on your guest list? I use this formula with my clients to help with making guest list decisions based on the total budget. This formula will tell you how many people to invite and stay within your budget. That formula is:

$$B(0.004)=GC$$

This formula allows you to have a food, beverage, stationery, and favor cost of $105 per person if you allocated 42% of your total budget to reception costs. Try it with any sized budget. It works! Take the guess work out of guest list management!

Homework Assignment: **When you determine your final guest count, begin compiling "A" and "B" lists. Those who are the "B" list can be invited if those on the "A" list RSVP they will not be in attendance.**

WEEK 5 – SHOP WITH PURPOSE

Welcome to week five of "Stylish Weddings & Things Guide to Developing Your Wedding Budget. Sticking to a budget is hard especially when you're planning one of the most momentous occasions of your lives. You will be tempted to buy in excess or get things simply because they're wedding related and you "must have it." Well to keep you on track here are some simple suggestions on how you can stay on track.

Create *a Shopping Schedule*

- Keep your budget with you at all times so you will be reminded of your limits
- Shop with purpose – when you're going shopping for your wedding, get what you intended to get and move on to the next item on your list.
- Plan to shop on a scheduled day. If you set a day to shop on Saturday, avoid making any purchases on any other day except for Saturday. If you feel like "you must have it," make note of it and get it on…Saturday.

Homework Assignment: **Finalize your wedding budget, use our shopping schedule at the end of this book and shop on purpose.**

WEEK 6 – BUDGET FRIENDLY WEDDING PROFESSIONALS

Welcome to week six of "Stylish Weddings & Things Guide to Developing Your Wedding Budget. Now that you are better prepared to conquer temptation by planning your shopping trips, let's get you prepared to shop and interview your prospective vendors aka your wedding team.

Choosing *Your Team*

Here are my top 8 must ask questions that are beneficial in preventing costly mistakes when choosing your wedding team. Prior to signing any agreements, make sure that any questions you have in addition to these are answered and you are left feeling confident that you will receive exceptional service.

1. How long have you been in business and are you licensed and insured?
2. What are your rates (including overtime and travel) and payment terms; what options are available to me for my budget?
3. What is your deposit requirement and is it refundable?
4. What is your cancellation and refund policy?
5. Who will be providing the actual services and what is your onsite dress code?
6. How long are you onsite?
7. What is your backup plan policy in case of illness or other emergencies preventing you from providing services?
8. Do you have a list of references?

Homework Assignment: **Come up with at least 3 more questions specific to each vendor's service offerings.**

WEEK 7 – ARE YOU DOING IT YOURSELF?

Welcome to week seven of "Stylish Weddings & Things Guide to Developing Your Wedding Budget." Planning your wedding should be a fun and exciting journey without having your nerves on edge, worrying if you made the right decisions or remembered every detail.

Let's begin our next topic…

When to do it yourself & *When to hire a pro*

With so many tasks and responsibilities that go into producing a wedding, some things should be handled by professionals. I agree that adding personal touches are the key to setting your wedding apart from others and to do so would require you to implement a few DIY projects. However, I urge you to seek (and pay for) the counsel of an expert professional prior to committing to taking on a DIY project.

With that said, here are my top **FOUR** indicators on when it's time to call a pro:

Call a Pro when:

1. You're making projects for a large guest list.

2. You don't have enough people volunteering to help you with your projects.

3. You or those helping you are not skilled in executing your projects.

4. You honestly can't devote the time and attention for your projects

Now, here are my top **THREE** recommendations on what you should neither do yourself nor hire an amateur for:

1. Catering – I wouldn't recommend you to prepare the menu yourself. Think about this for a second: Do you really want to deal with the kitchen, staff (you'll need hands to help serve), food replenishment, etc. all while hosting your wedding? I would also leave this important task to an experienced catering professional because of certain liabilities involved such as insurance and licenses for food handling and serving alcohol.

2. Photography – Don't gamble on an amateur who's using your special day to build their portfolio. Hire an experienced and skill photographer who is diverse in their shooting style and (important) has a second shooter to capture even more special moments and who serves as their back up.

3. Entertainment – The entertainment is what's going to set the tone for your celebration. You want to make sure that you and your guests are having a good time and whether or not you decide to hire a DJ or Band, do hire a real person experienced in playing weddings who can keep your guests entertained and having a great experience. If your budget doesn't cover the cost to hire a professional to entertain, consult with one and pay to have them create a playlist, load it into your MP3 player, and assign someone in your bridal party to be responsible for playback and troubleshooting.

Side Note: Hiring an Officiant is a personal choice. This person should be someone you trust will perform your wedding ceremony with the highest of highest level of professionalism and respect of your wishes. If you choose to delegate this important task to a friend or family member, I recommend you suggest they practice, practice, and practice some more – even if they're professional public speakers. Officiating a wedding bears the responsibility of legally uniting a couple and your Officiant will want to make sure he gets it right the first time.

Homework Assignment: **Make a list of elements you intend to turn into DIY projects and determine whether or not you or your family and friends, have the appropriate skillset and time to accomplish them. If not, seek professional assistance.**

Welcome to week eight of the "Stylish Weddings & Things Guide to Developing Your Wedding Budget." We've talked about what you should ask prior to booking your wedding professionals. Now we're going to talk a bit about negotiating with them to get the best services your budget can afford.

Let's begin our next topic…

"Value increases are better than service discounts!"

Prior to meeting with any wedding professional, you already know how much you can afford, but you don't know "what" you can afford. Your wedding professional has a menu of products and/or services already in place and can help you determine what you can afford. But what if what you can afford is not what you want? What if you really want the most expensive product/service offered? What would be your plan to get what you want? If the first thing that came to mind is to ask for a discount, don't do it and here's why. You are more likely to receive added value than to receive a discount for services. What's the difference? Let me put it in perspective:

How would you feel if you went on a job interview and the employer said to you:

> *"Your resume is outstanding and you're more than qualified to fill this position for the salary you want, however we saw another candidate who has the same experience and qualifications who offered to accept the position for less money than that of your salary requirements. If you want the job, you will need to reduce your salary requirements."*

That would NOT go over well with you would it? What is your immediate reaction to this statement?

Now suppose the employer said to you in the same situation:

> *"Your resume is outstanding and you're more than qualified to fill this position for the salary you want, however we saw another candidate who has the same experience and qualifications who offered to accept the position for less money than that of your salary requirements. The job is yours but we'll need you to also take on additional duties with this position."*

Much better right?

"Vendors will be happy to extend more value in a service than to offer you a discount."

Wedding professionals want to give you a product and/or service that will leave you more than satisfied and they can't do that if they're giving you discounts. Giving you discounts usually mean they will need to cut corners to make up the difference which usually results in delivering a poor quality service and leaving you disappointed at the end of the day – and not just any day, YOUR WEDDING DAY. Instead, tell your intended wedding professional what you love about the service you "can't afford" and ask if they would be able to give you something similar for the price you can afford. However, if you're not satisfied with the custom version of services with the value add, then ask the wedding professional for a referral and allow them to connect you with a service provider who is a match for your budget.

Homework Assignment: If you've budgeted for a service but can't afford the price tag, revisit your priorities list and determine if you need to modify your budget. Remember, the point of the priorities list is to help you make buying decisions based on what you absolutely must have versus what would be nice to have, but can live without.

Welcome to week nine of the "Stylish Weddings & Things Guide to Developing Your Wedding Budget." Planning your wedding should be a fun and exciting journey without having your nerves on edge, worrying if you made the right decisions or remembered every detail.

Let's begin our next topic…

Save more than just *A Few Dollars*

Here are my top **EIGHT** money savers in planning a wedding within a $10,000 budget.

1. Keep your guest count small as I mentioned in week four. The more people you invite, the more food, the more alcohol (big expense), the more tables, the more favors, the more centerpieces, the more…get my drift? Use our formula for determining a budget friendly guest count, B (Budget) x .004 = GC (Guest Count)

2. Keep your bridal party small. Having a Maid/Matron of Honor and Best Man alone will make a lovely processional. Also with a small bridal party, you will be saving on other expenses such as flowers, gifts, food & beverages, and favors. Or you can exclude having a bridal party altogether for even more savings.

3. Consider buying a dress off the rack at department stores, consignment shops, and vintage boutique shops. Don't over rule searching for your gown at formal wear dress shops that aren't "bridal." Visit trunk shows and sample sales. You may even discover that a recently wedded bride is willing to part with her designer gown for a lot less than you'd pay at a boutique. Check the popular wedding websites for their bride discussion forums or your newspaper's classified.

4. Marry off season between the months of November and April. Many wedding professionals and businesses are not usually busy around this time (with the exception of the major holiday parties) and you may be able to save significantly on costs as opposed to marrying during wedding peak season May-October.

5. Marry during the week or on a Sunday. Stay away from Saturday weddings as this is a premium and expensive choice. You may shudder at the idea of getting married on a

weeknight and feel your guests may not show up. However, if planned well by issuing save the dates prior to sending out your invitations, your guests will appreciate the heads up and will make arrangements to celebrate with you. Sunday weddings are also popular choices to consider if you want to save on wedding costs because it's also considered a week night and most reception hall facilities are not busy during this time nor are most wedding vendors.

6. Ask your friends for help if they have an expertise in certain components of your wedding. Don't be shy to ask them for help because a lot of times they'll be more than happy to roll up their sleeves and help *(make sure to give them a special note of thanks when you come back from your honeymoon!)*.

7. Consider other banquet/catering options that are not "wedding" related. You will find a significant savings of 20% or more in some areas by opting for a non-wedding food service. This is also a good rule of thumb when shopping for any of your wedding services, think of non-wedding alternatives and you can save a fortune. The reason why the savings are big is because the work involved in producing a wedding is more detailed and intricate than any other special occasion.

8. Have an early morning service with a breakfast, brunch, or luncheon reception to shave costs by not serving premium dinner menu options. You'll also save on alcohol as most people won't drink heavily during the day.

Welcome to week 10 which concludes "Stylish Weddings & Things Guide to Developing Your Wedding Budget." I hope you feel confident that you will be able to stay within your budget and therefore aid in relieving some of the stress you may be feeling during the planning process.

Let's begin our final topic…

Honeymoon Planning *A bit of advice*

Avoid honeymoon packages and travel as regular vacationers. The difference in this is you'll save a hefty penny to the tune of hundreds (or thousands) of dollars. Some of the perks included with honeymoon packages involve a lot of personal attention to you as a couple such as butler services and private, intimate activities designed for newlyweds. Even as regular vacationers, all inclusive options are only as good to you as the benefits included. Discover activities are included with your vacation or honeymoon package and determine if you're really going to use everything they offer. If not, negotiate perk options that will include only what you intend to use.

Homework Assignment: **Speak to a travel agent about how to reduce your costs by eliminating activities and/or services you won't be using.**

Thank you for reading "Stylish Weddings & Things Guide to Developing Your Wedding Budget." Have you gone shopping armed with the tools you received so far? How did you do? What challenges are you still facing? Let me know by writing to hotline@stylishweddingsandthings.com. I do hope you've enjoyed it and are now empowered with the tools to save and plan a budget friendly stylish wedding.

Reward Yourself, *You Deserve it*

If you are able to come under budget in any of your wedding expenses, cheers! I toast to your victory and encourage you to reward yourself by taking your savings and increase the budget wherever your heart desires and get those items you wouldn't have been able to get otherwise. Or buy yourself something amazing as a reminder of a job well done in coming under budget.

Homework Assignment: **Give yourself an extra reward if you were able to get something for nothing, like a friend who's offering a service as a gift! Free is always in budget.**

I want to congratulate you again on your engagement and it is my wish for you to enjoy this time with each other on your journey to a long lasting marriage. Should you have any other questions or concerns with your wedding planning efforts, drop me a line at (862) 248-2555 or let me know by writing to hotline@stylishweddingsandthings.com

Week 1 – Bank Comparison Table

Bank Comparison Table

Wedding Planning Friendly Features	Bank	Bank	Bank
Interest Bearing Checking Accounts			
Debit Card Rewards Program			
Direct Deposit			
Online Bill Pay Services			
Overdraft Protection Services			
Mobile Banking Services			
Mobile Phone Check Deposits			
Mobile Phone Money Transfers			
Other:			

Budget Priorities Checklist

Use this form to rate the details that will make your wedding unique to you.

Part One – First begin prioritizing the core essentials.

Wedding Essentials	Must Have	Love to Have	Like to Have	Can Do Without	No Way
Ceremony	☐	☐	☐	☐	☐
Reception	☐	☐	☐	☐	☐
Caterer	☐	☐	☐	☐	☐
Photographer	☐	☐	☐	☐	☐
Videographer	☐	☐	☐	☐	☐
Entertainment	☐	☐	☐	☐	☐
Stationery	☐	☐	☐	☐	☐
Transportation	☐	☐	☐	☐	☐
Attire	☐	☐	☐	☐	☐
Beauty Services	☐	☐	☐	☐	☐
Wedding Cake	☐	☐	☐	☐	☐
Favors/Gifts	☐	☐	☐	☐	☐
Honeymoon	☐	☐	☐	☐	☐

Part Two – Prioritize the details within each wedding essential. Add your own list of details and rate them accordingly.

Ceremony	Must have	Love to Have	Like to Have	Can Do Without	No Way
Officiant/Celebrant/Clergy	☐				
Location – Indoors	☐	☐	☐	☐	☐
Location - Outdoors	☐	☐	☐	☐	☐
Transportation	☐	☐	☐	☐	☐
Backdrops	☐	☐	☐	☐	☐
Candles	☐	☐	☐	☐	☐
Traditional Rituals	☐	☐	☐	☐	☐
Unity Candle, Broom, Other Unity Props	☐	☐	☐	☐	☐
Aisle Runner	☐	☐	☐	☐	☐
Pew Decorations	☐	☐	☐	☐	☐
Alter Decorations	☐	☐	☐	☐	☐
Writing Vows	☐	☐	☐	☐	☐
Wedding Programs	☐	☐	☐	☐	☐
Receiving Line	☐	☐	☐	☐	☐
Guest book	☐	☐	☐	☐	☐
Ceremony Music	☐	☐	☐	☐	☐
Flower Girl Basket	☐	☐	☐	☐	☐
Ring Pillow	☐	☐	☐	☐	☐
Bouquets, Boutonnieres, and other personal flowers	☐	☐	☐	☐	☐
Outdoor Signage	☐	☐	☐	☐	☐
Bridesmaids & Groomsmen	☐	☐	☐	☐	☐

Ceremony	Must have	Love to Have	Like to Have	Can Do Without	No Way
	☐	☐	☐	☐	☐
	☐	☐	☐	☐	☐
	☐	☐	☐	☐	☐
	☐	☐	☐	☐	☐
	☐	☐	☐	☐	☐
	☐	☐	☐	☐	☐
	☐	☐	☐	☐	☐
	☐	☐	☐	☐	☐
	☐	☐	☐	☐	☐
	☐	☐	☐	☐	☐
	☐	☐	☐	☐	☐
	☐	☐	☐	☐	☐
	☐	☐	☐	☐	☐
	☐	☐	☐	☐	☐
	☐	☐	☐	☐	☐
	☐	☐	☐	☐	☐
	☐	☐	☐	☐	☐
	☐	☐	☐	☐	☐
	☐	☐	☐	☐	☐
	☐	☐	☐	☐	☐
	☐	☐	☐	☐	☐
	☐	☐	☐	☐	☐

Reception	Must Have	Love to Have	Like to Have	Can Do Without	No Way
Location – Indoors	☐	☐	☐	☐	☐
Location – Outdoors	☐	☐	☐	☐	☐
Cocktail Reception	☐	☐	☐	☐	☐
Buffet Service	☐	☐	☐	☐	☐
Seated/Plated Service	☐	☐	☐	☐	☐
Modern	☐	☐	☐	☐	☐
Vintage/Historic	☐	☐	☐	☐	☐
Rustic	☐	☐	☐	☐	☐
All Inclusive	☐	☐	☐	☐	☐
Flowers	☐	☐	☐	☐	☐
Candles	☐	☐	☐	☐	☐
Premium Linens	☐	☐	☐	☐	☐
DJ	☐	☐	☐	☐	☐
Band	☐	☐	☐	☐	☐
Centerpieces	☐	☐	☐	☐	☐
Ice Sculptures	☐	☐	☐	☐	☐
Photo booth	☐	☐	☐	☐	☐
Favors	☐	☐	☐	☐	☐
Novelty Items (ex: Props)	☐	☐	☐	☐	☐
Entertainment (ex: Live performers)	☐	☐	☐	☐	☐
Childcare	☐	☐	☐	☐	☐
Overnight	☐	☐	☐	☐	☐

Reception – Fill in any other details	Must Have	Love to Have	Like to Have	Can Do Without	No Way
	☐	☐	☐	☐	☐
	☐	☐	☐	☐	☐
	☐	☐	☐	☐	☐
	☐	☐	☐	☐	☐
	☐	☐	☐	☐	☐
	☐	☐	☐	☐	☐
	☐	☐	☐	☐	☐
	☐	☐	☐	☐	☐
	☐	☐	☐	☐	☐
	☐	☐	☐	☐	☐
	☐	☐	☐	☐	☐
	☐	☐	☐	☐	☐
	☐	☐	☐	☐	☐
	☐	☐	☐	☐	☐
	☐	☐	☐	☐	☐
	☐	☐	☐	☐	☐
	☐	☐	☐	☐	☐
	☐	☐	☐	☐	☐
	☐	☐	☐	☐	☐
	☐	☐	☐	☐	☐
	☐	☐	☐	☐	☐

Food & Beverage	Must Have	Love to Have	Like to Have	Can Do Without	No Way

Cocktail Hour
  □ Butler served hors d'oeuvres
  □ Hors d'oeuvres stations
	□	□	□	□	□

Buffet Service
  □ Staffed/Servers
  □ Food Stations
  □ Self Service
	□	□	□	□	□

Sit Down Service	□	□	□	□	□
Family Style Service	□	□	□	□	□
Soup/Salad	□	□	□	□	□
Pasta	□	□	□	□	□
Beef	□	□	□	□	□
Chicken	□	□	□	□	□
Pork	□	□	□	□	□
Fish	□	□	□	□	□
Lamb	□	□	□	□	□
Vegetarian	□	□	□	□	□
Ethnic Cuisine:_____	□	□	□	□	□
Kosher	□	□	□	□	□
Vegan	□	□	□	□	□
Gluten Free	□	□	□	□	□

Bar Options
  □ Open
  □ Limited
  □ Cash Bar
	□	□	□	□	□

Wine	□	□	□	□	□
Beer	□	□	□	□	□
Signature Drink	□	□	□	□	□
Champagne	□	□	□	□	□

Food & Beverage – Fill in any other details	Must Have	Love to Have	Like to Have	Can Do Without	No Way
	☐	☐	☐	☐	☐
	☐	☐	☐	☐	☐
	☐	☐	☐	☐	☐
	☐	☐	☐	☐	☐
	☐	☐	☐	☐	☐
	☐	☐	☐	☐	☐
	☐	☐	☐	☐	☐
	☐	☐	☐	☐	☐
	☐	☐	☐	☐	☐
	☐	☐	☐	☐	☐
	☐	☐	☐	☐	☐
	☐	☐	☐	☐	☐
	☐	☐	☐	☐	☐
	☐	☐	☐	☐	☐
	☐	☐	☐	☐	☐
	☐	☐	☐	☐	☐
	☐	☐	☐	☐	☐
	☐	☐	☐	☐	☐
	☐	☐	☐	☐	☐
	☐	☐	☐	☐	☐
	☐	☐	☐	☐	☐
	☐	☐	☐	☐	☐

Photographer	Must Have	Love to Have	Like to Have	Can Do Without	No Way
Photojournalism	☐	☐	☐	☐	☐
Traditional	☐	☐	☐	☐	☐
Artistic	☐	☐	☐	☐	☐
Natural Light	☐	☐	☐	☐	☐
Boudoir	☐	☐	☐	☐	☐
Story book	☐	☐	☐	☐	☐
Modern	☐	☐	☐	☐	☐
Hollywood/Celebrity	☐	☐	☐	☐	☐
Special Visual Effects	☐	☐	☐	☐	☐
Engagement Sessions	☐	☐	☐	☐	☐
Photo Albums	☐	☐	☐	☐	☐
DVD	☐	☐	☐	☐	☐
Thank You Cards	☐	☐	☐	☐	☐
	☐	☐	☐	☐	☐
	☐	☐	☐	☐	☐
	☐	☐	☐	☐	☐
	☐	☐	☐	☐	☐
	☐	☐	☐	☐	☐
	☐	☐	☐	☐	☐
	☐	☐	☐	☐	☐
	☐	☐	☐	☐	☐
	☐	☐	☐	☐	☐

Photographer – Fill in any other details	Must Have	Love to Have	Like to Have	Can Do Without	No Way
	☐	☐	☐	☐	☐
	☐	☐	☐	☐	☐
	☐	☐	☐	☐	☐
	☐	☐	☐	☐	☐
	☐	☐	☐	☐	☐
	☐	☐	☐	☐	☐
	☐	☐	☐	☐	☐
	☐	☐	☐	☐	☐
	☐	☐	☐	☐	☐
	☐	☐	☐	☐	☐
	☐	☐	☐	☐	☐
	☐	☐	☐	☐	☐
	☐	☐	☐	☐	☐
	☐	☐	☐	☐	☐
	☐	☐	☐	☐	☐
	☐	☐	☐	☐	☐
	☐	☐	☐	☐	☐
	☐	☐	☐	☐	☐
	☐	☐	☐	☐	☐
	☐	☐	☐	☐	☐
	☐	☐	☐	☐	☐
	☐	☐	☐	☐	☐

Videographer	Must Have	Love to Have	Like to Have	Can Do Without	No Way
Journalistic	☐	☐	☐	☐	☐
Cinematic	☐	☐	☐	☐	☐
Storytelling	☐	☐	☐	☐	☐
Traditional/Raw	☐	☐	☐	☐	☐
Romantic	☐	☐	☐	☐	☐
Modern	☐	☐	☐	☐	☐
Edgy	☐	☐	☐	☐	☐
DVD	☐	☐	☐	☐	☐
Blue Ray	☐	☐	☐	☐	☐
	☐	☐	☐	☐	☐
	☐	☐	☐	☐	☐
	☐	☐	☐	☐	☐
	☐	☐	☐	☐	☐
	☐	☐	☐	☐	☐
	☐	☐	☐	☐	☐
	☐	☐	☐	☐	☐
	☐	☐	☐	☐	☐
	☐	☐	☐	☐	☐
	☐	☐	☐	☐	☐
	☐	☐	☐	☐	☐
	☐	☐	☐	☐	☐
	☐	☐	☐	☐	☐

Videographer – Fill in any other details	Must Have	Love to Have	Like to Have	Can Do Without	No Way
	☐	☐	☐	☐	☐
	☐	☐	☐	☐	☐
	☐	☐	☐	☐	☐
	☐	☐	☐	☐	☐
	☐	☐	☐	☐	☐
	☐	☐	☐	☐	☐
	☐	☐	☐	☐	☐
	☐	☐	☐	☐	☐
	☐	☐	☐	☐	☐
	☐	☐	☐	☐	☐
	☐	☐	☐	☐	☐
	☐	☐	☐	☐	☐
	☐	☐	☐	☐	☐
	☐	☐	☐	☐	☐
	☐	☐	☐	☐	☐
	☐	☐	☐	☐	☐
	☐	☐	☐	☐	☐
	☐	☐	☐	☐	☐
	☐	☐	☐	☐	☐
	☐	☐	☐	☐	☐
	☐	☐	☐	☐	☐

Entertainment	Must Have	Love to Have	Like to Have	Can Do Without	No Way
Band	☐	☐	☐	☐	☐
DJ	☐	☐	☐	☐	☐
Solo Artist / Vocalist	☐	☐	☐	☐	☐
Comedian	☐	☐	☐	☐	☐
Impersonators	☐	☐	☐	☐	☐
Karaoke	☐	☐	☐	☐	☐
Classic Ensembles	☐	☐	☐	☐	☐
R&B/Hip Hop	☐	☐	☐	☐	☐
Jazz	☐	☐	☐	☐	☐
Swing	☐	☐	☐	☐	☐
Rock	☐	☐	☐	☐	☐
Dance/Pop	☐	☐	☐	☐	☐
Disco/80's	☐	☐	☐	☐	☐
Dancers / Performers	☐	☐	☐	☐	☐
Guests Interaction	☐	☐	☐	☐	☐
Gobo	☐	☐	☐	☐	☐
Up Lighting	☐	☐	☐	☐	☐
Fog Machine	☐	☐	☐	☐	☐
	☐	☐	☐	☐	☐
	☐	☐	☐	☐	☐
	☐	☐	☐	☐	☐
	☐	☐	☐	☐	☐

Entertainment – Fill in any other details	Must Have	Love to Have	Like to Have	Can Do Without	No Way
	☐	☐	☐	☐	☐
	☐	☐	☐	☐	☐
	☐	☐	☐	☐	☐
	☐	☐	☐	☐	☐
	☐	☐	☐	☐	☐
	☐	☐	☐	☐	☐
	☐	☐	☐	☐	☐
	☐	☐	☐	☐	☐
	☐	☐	☐	☐	☐
	☐	☐	☐	☐	☐
	☐	☐	☐	☐	☐
	☐	☐	☐	☐	☐
	☐	☐	☐	☐	☐
	☐	☐	☐	☐	☐
	☐	☐	☐	☐	☐
	☐	☐	☐	☐	☐
	☐	☐	☐	☐	☐
	☐	☐	☐	☐	☐
	☐	☐	☐	☐	☐
	☐	☐	☐	☐	☐
	☐	☐	☐	☐	☐
	☐	☐	☐	☐	☐

Stationery	Must Have	Love to Have	Like to Have	Can Do Without	No Way
Invitations	☐	☐	☐	☐	☐
Save-the-Dates	☐	☐	☐	☐	☐
Wedding Announcements	☐	☐	☐	☐	☐
Seating Assignments	☐	☐	☐	☐	☐
Menus	☐	☐	☐	☐	☐
Wedding Programs	☐	☐	☐	☐	☐
Table Numbers	☐	☐	☐	☐	☐
Escort Cards	☐	☐	☐	☐	☐
Place Cards	☐	☐	☐	☐	☐
Thank you cards	☐	☐	☐	☐	☐
Embellishments	☐	☐	☐	☐	☐
Calligrapher	☐	☐	☐	☐	☐
Wedding stamps	☐	☐	☐	☐	☐
	☐	☐	☐	☐	☐
	☐	☐	☐	☐	☐
	☐	☐	☐	☐	☐
	☐	☐	☐	☐	☐
	☐	☐	☐	☐	☐
	☐	☐	☐	☐	☐
	☐	☐	☐	☐	☐
	☐	☐	☐	☐	☐
	☐	☐	☐	☐	☐

Stationery – Fill in any other details	Must Have	Love to Have	Like to Have	Can Do Without	No Way
	☐	☐	☐	☐	☐
	☐	☐	☐	☐	☐
	☐	☐	☐	☐	☐
	☐	☐	☐	☐	☐
	☐	☐	☐	☐	☐
	☐	☐	☐	☐	☐
	☐	☐	☐	☐	☐
	☐	☐	☐	☐	☐
	☐	☐	☐	☐	☐
	☐	☐	☐	☐	☐
	☐	☐	☐	☐	☐
	☐	☐	☐	☐	☐
	☐	☐	☐	☐	☐
	☐	☐	☐	☐	☐
	☐	☐	☐	☐	☐
	☐	☐	☐	☐	☐
	☐	☐	☐	☐	☐
	☐	☐	☐	☐	☐
	☐	☐	☐	☐	☐
	☐	☐	☐	☐	☐
	☐	☐	☐	☐	☐
	☐	☐	☐	☐	☐

Transportation	Must Have	Love to Have	Like to Have	Can Do Without	No Way
Limo	☐	☐	☐	☐	☐
Party Bus	☐	☐	☐	☐	☐
Stretch SUV	☐	☐	☐	☐	☐
Antique Car	☐	☐	☐	☐	☐
Town Car	☐	☐	☐	☐	☐
Horse & Carriage	☐	☐	☐	☐	☐
Helicopter	☐	☐	☐	☐	☐
Air Balloon	☐	☐	☐	☐	☐
Chauffer	☐	☐	☐	☐	☐
Stocked Bar	☐	☐	☐	☐	☐
Entertainment System	☐	☐	☐	☐	☐
Red Carpet	☐	☐	☐	☐	☐
	☐	☐	☐	☐	☐
	☐	☐	☐	☐	☐
	☐	☐	☐	☐	☐
	☐	☐	☐	☐	☐
	☐	☐	☐	☐	☐
	☐	☐	☐	☐	☐
	☐	☐	☐	☐	☐
	☐	☐	☐	☐	☐
	☐	☐	☐	☐	☐
	☐	☐	☐	☐	☐

Transportation – Fill in any other details	Must Have	Love to Have	Like to Have	Can Do Without	No Way
	☐	☐	☐	☐	☐
	☐	☐	☐	☐	☐
	☐	☐	☐	☐	☐
	☐	☐	☐	☐	☐
	☐	☐	☐	☐	☐
	☐	☐	☐	☐	☐
	☐	☐	☐	☐	☐
	☐	☐	☐	☐	☐
	☐	☐	☐	☐	☐
	☐	☐	☐	☐	☐
	☐	☐	☐	☐	☐
	☐	☐	☐	☐	☐
	☐	☐	☐	☐	☐
	☐	☐	☐	☐	☐
	☐	☐	☐	☐	☐
	☐	☐	☐	☐	☐
	☐	☐	☐	☐	☐
	☐	☐	☐	☐	☐
	☐	☐	☐	☐	☐
	☐	☐	☐	☐	☐
	☐	☐	☐	☐	☐

Attire	Must Have	Love to Have	Like to Have	Can Do Without	No Way
Designer	☐	☐	☐	☐	☐
Off the Rack	☐	☐	☐	☐	☐
Custom	☐	☐	☐	☐	☐
Elegant	☐	☐	☐	☐	☐
Regal	☐	☐	☐	☐	☐
Sexy	☐	☐	☐	☐	☐
Grandeur	☐	☐	☐	☐	☐
Simple	☐	☐	☐	☐	☐
Form fitting	☐	☐	☐	☐	☐
Light & Airy	☐	☐	☐	☐	☐
Color	☐	☐	☐	☐	☐
Light	☐	☐	☐	☐	☐
Men: Suit	☐	☐	☐	☐	☐
Men: Tuxedo	☐	☐	☐	☐	☐
	☐	☐	☐	☐	☐
	☐	☐	☐	☐	☐
	☐	☐	☐	☐	☐
	☐	☐	☐	☐	☐
	☐	☐	☐	☐	☐
	☐	☐	☐	☐	☐
	☐	☐	☐	☐	☐
	☐	☐	☐	☐	☐

Attire – Fill in any other details	Must Have	Love to Have	Like to Have	Can Do Without	No Way
	☐	☐	☐	☐	☐
	☐	☐	☐	☐	☐
	☐	☐	☐	☐	☐
	☐	☐	☐	☐	☐
	☐	☐	☐	☐	☐
	☐	☐	☐	☐	☐
	☐	☐	☐	☐	☐
	☐	☐	☐	☐	☐
	☐	☐	☐	☐	☐
	☐	☐	☐	☐	☐
	☐	☐	☐	☐	☐
	☐	☐	☐	☐	☐
	☐	☐	☐	☐	☐
	☐	☐	☐	☐	☐
	☐	☐	☐	☐	☐
	☐	☐	☐	☐	☐
	☐	☐	☐	☐	☐
	☐	☐	☐	☐	☐
	☐	☐	☐	☐	☐
	☐	☐	☐	☐	☐
	☐	☐	☐	☐	☐
	☐	☐	☐	☐	☐

Beauty Services	Must Have	Love to Have	Like to Have	Can Do Without	No Way
Make Up: Traditional	☐	☐	☐	☐	☐
Make Up: Air Brush	☐	☐	☐	☐	☐
Eyelash Application	☐	☐	☐	☐	☐
Spa Services	☐	☐	☐	☐	☐
Hair Cut	☐	☐	☐	☐	☐
Up Do	☐	☐	☐	☐	☐
Braid	☐	☐	☐	☐	☐
Hair Piece/Veil	☐	☐	☐	☐	☐
Blow Out	☐	☐	☐	☐	☐
	☐	☐	☐	☐	☐
	☐	☐	☐	☐	☐
	☐	☐	☐	☐	☐
	☐	☐	☐	☐	☐
	☐	☐	☐	☐	☐
	☐	☐	☐	☐	☐
	☐	☐	☐	☐	☐
	☐	☐	☐	☐	☐
	☐	☐	☐	☐	☐
	☐	☐	☐	☐	☐
	☐	☐	☐	☐	☐
	☐	☐	☐	☐	☐
	☐	☐	☐	☐	☐

Beauty Services – Fill in any other details	Must Have	Love to Have	Like to Have	Can Do Without	No Way
	☐	☐	☐	☐	☐
	☐	☐	☐	☐	☐
	☐	☐	☐	☐	☐
	☐	☐	☐	☐	☐
	☐	☐	☐	☐	☐
	☐	☐	☐	☐	☐
	☐	☐	☐	☐	☐
	☐	☐	☐	☐	☐
	☐	☐	☐	☐	☐
	☐	☐	☐	☐	☐
	☐	☐	☐	☐	☐
	☐	☐	☐	☐	☐
	☐	☐	☐	☐	☐
	☐	☐	☐	☐	☐
	☐	☐	☐	☐	☐
	☐	☐	☐	☐	☐
	☐	☐	☐	☐	☐
	☐	☐	☐	☐	☐
	☐	☐	☐	☐	☐
	☐	☐	☐	☐	☐
	☐	☐	☐	☐	☐
	☐	☐	☐	☐	☐

Wedding Cake	Must Have	Love to Have	Like to Have	Can Do Without	No Way
Multi-tier	☐	☐	☐	☐	☐
Sheet	☐	☐	☐	☐	☐
Round	☐	☐	☐	☐	☐
Square	☐	☐	☐	☐	☐
Mad Hatter (Twisted Cake)	☐	☐	☐	☐	☐
Sweet	☐	☐	☐	☐	☐
Fondant	☐	☐	☐	☐	☐
Butter Crème	☐	☐	☐	☐	☐
Whipped Crème	☐	☐	☐	☐	☐
Grooms Cake	☐	☐	☐	☐	☐
Sugar Flowers	☐	☐	☐	☐	☐
Real/Silk Flowers	☐	☐	☐	☐	☐
Intricate Design	☐	☐	☐	☐	☐
Simple Design	☐	☐	☐	☐	☐
Cake Topper	☐	☐	☐	☐	☐
Cupcakes	☐	☐	☐	☐	☐
	☐	☐	☐	☐	☐
	☐	☐	☐	☐	☐
	☐	☐	☐	☐	☐
	☐	☐	☐	☐	☐
	☐	☐	☐	☐	☐
	☐	☐	☐	☐	☐

Wedding Cake – Fill in any other details	Must Have	Love to Have	Like to Have	Can Do Without	No Way
	☐	☐	☐	☐	☐
	☐	☐	☐	☐	☐
	☐	☐	☐	☐	☐
	☐	☐	☐	☐	☐
	☐	☐	☐	☐	☐
	☐	☐	☐	☐	☐
	☐	☐	☐	☐	☐
	☐	☐	☐	☐	☐
	☐	☐	☐	☐	☐
	☐	☐	☐	☐	☐
	☐	☐	☐	☐	☐
	☐	☐	☐	☐	☐
	☐	☐	☐	☐	☐
	☐	☐	☐	☐	☐
	☐	☐	☐	☐	☐
	☐	☐	☐	☐	☐
	☐	☐	☐	☐	☐
	☐	☐	☐	☐	☐
	☐	☐	☐	☐	☐
	☐	☐	☐	☐	☐
	☐	☐	☐	☐	☐
	☐	☐	☐	☐	☐

Favors/Gifts	Must Have	Love to Have	Like to Have	Can Do Without	No Way
Seasonal	☐	☐	☐	☐	☐
Functional	☐	☐	☐	☐	☐
Disposable	☐	☐	☐	☐	☐
Donation	☐	☐	☐	☐	☐
Candy	☐	☐	☐	☐	☐
Plants	☐	☐	☐	☐	☐
Photos	☐	☐	☐	☐	☐
Frames	☐	☐	☐	☐	☐
Gender Specific	☐	☐	☐	☐	☐
Children	☐	☐	☐	☐	☐
Family	☐	☐	☐	☐	☐
	☐	☐	☐	☐	☐
	☐	☐	☐	☐	☐
	☐	☐	☐	☐	☐
	☐	☐	☐	☐	☐
	☐	☐	☐	☐	☐
	☐	☐	☐	☐	☐
	☐	☐	☐	☐	☐
	☐	☐	☐	☐	☐
	☐	☐	☐	☐	☐
	☐	☐	☐	☐	☐
	☐	☐	☐	☐	☐

Favors/Gifts – Fill in any other details	Must Have	Love to Have	Like to Have	Can Do Without	No Way
	☐	☐	☐	☐	☐
	☐	☐	☐	☐	☐
	☐	☐	☐	☐	☐
	☐	☐	☐	☐	☐
	☐	☐	☐	☐	☐
	☐	☐	☐	☐	☐
	☐	☐	☐	☐	☐
	☐	☐	☐	☐	☐
	☐	☐	☐	☐	☐
	☐	☐	☐	☐	☐
	☐	☐	☐	☐	☐
	☐	☐	☐	☐	☐
	☐	☐	☐	☐	☐
	☐	☐	☐	☐	☐
	☐	☐	☐	☐	☐
	☐	☐	☐	☐	☐
	☐	☐	☐	☐	☐
	☐	☐	☐	☐	☐
	☐	☐	☐	☐	☐
	☐	☐	☐	☐	☐
	☐	☐	☐	☐	☐
	☐	☐	☐	☐	☐
	☐	☐	☐	☐	☐

Honeymoon	Must Have	Love to Have	Like to Have	Can Do Without	No Way
Domestic	☐	☐	☐	☐	☐
International	☐	☐	☐	☐	☐
Beach	☐	☐	☐	☐	☐
Guided Tours	☐	☐	☐	☐	☐
Resorts	☐	☐	☐	☐	☐
Cruise	☐	☐	☐	☐	☐
Adventure	☐	☐	☐	☐	☐
Spa	☐	☐	☐	☐	☐
Golf	☐	☐	☐	☐	☐
Swimming	☐	☐	☐	☐	☐
Relaxation	☐	☐	☐	☐	☐
Cultural	☐	☐	☐	☐	☐
Historic	☐	☐	☐	☐	☐
	☐	☐	☐	☐	☐
	☐	☐	☐	☐	☐
	☐	☐	☐	☐	☐
	☐	☐	☐	☐	☐
	☐	☐	☐	☐	☐
	☐	☐	☐	☐	☐
	☐	☐	☐	☐	☐
	☐	☐	☐	☐	☐
	☐	☐	☐	☐	☐

Honeymoon – Fill in any other details	Must Have	Love to Have	Like to Have	Can Do Without	No Way
	☐	☐	☐	☐	☐
	☐	☐	☐	☐	☐
	☐	☐	☐	☐	☐
	☐	☐	☐	☐	☐
	☐	☐	☐	☐	☐
	☐	☐	☐	☐	☐
	☐	☐	☐	☐	☐
	☐	☐	☐	☐	☐
	☐	☐	☐	☐	☐
	☐	☐	☐	☐	☐
	☐	☐	☐	☐	☐
	☐	☐	☐	☐	☐
	☐	☐	☐	☐	☐
	☐	☐	☐	☐	☐
	☐	☐	☐	☐	☐
	☐	☐	☐	☐	☐
	☐	☐	☐	☐	☐
	☐	☐	☐	☐	☐
	☐	☐	☐	☐	☐
	☐	☐	☐	☐	☐
	☐	☐	☐	☐	☐
	☐	☐	☐	☐	☐

Wedding Budget Planner

Use this planner as a guide along with your priorities checklist to determine who will pay for which wedding expense and how much they will commit to. When you've completed this, you will have a clear view of what your overall budget will be.

Wedding Expense	Who Pays	Budget
Pre-Wedding Parties		
• Rehearsal Dinner	_____	$_____
• Out-of-Towner's Brunch	_____	$_____
Stationery		
• Invitations & Announcements, Programs, etc.	_____	$_____
Attire		
• Bridal Gown, accessories, undergarments	_____	$_____
• Groom's formal wear	_____	$_____
Photography/Videographer	_____	$_____
Flowers & Decorations	_____	$_____
Ceremony		
• Church/location fees, organists, etc.	_____	$_____
• Marriage license & Officiant	_____	$_____

Wedding Expense	Who Pays	Budget
Reception • Venue • Food & Beverage • Wedding cake • Rental Items	_____ _____ _____ _____	$_____ $_____ $_____ $_____
Entertainment	_____	$_____
Favors/Gifts	_____	$_____
Transportation	_____	$_____
Honeymoon	_____	$_____
	Total Budget	$_____

Wedding Budget

Category	Budget	Quotes	Difference	% of Budget
Ceremony				3.00%
Stationery				2.50%
Wedding Rings				2.00%
Attire & Grooming				5.00%
Photography Videography				8.00%
Flowers/Décor				7.00%
Reception				40.00%
Music/Entertainment				7.50%
Transportation				2.00%
Gifts				3.00%
Wedding Planner				10.00%
Honeymoon				7.00%
Miscellaneous				3.00%
Total Budget				100.0%

Shopping Schedule

Use this shopping schedule to plan out your shopping days. Make several copies for each week.

Week _____

Shopping Days	What am I shopping for?	How much money do I have to spend today?	Store	Start Time	End Time
Sunday					
Monday					
Tuesday					
Wednesday					
Thursday					
Friday					
Saturday					

www.ingramcontent.com/pod-product-compliance
Lightning Source LLC
Chambersburg PA
CBHW041513280526
45792CB00004B/1243